What others are saying ...

Love it! I recommend this book to anyone wanting a new understanding and a fresh touch of God the Father's love.
Daphne Godwin, Ffald Y Brenin,
Place of 'The Grace Outpouring'

This book will draw you into a deep longing for intimacy with Father God. I was very touched by the depth and richness of relationship between Eve and Papa.
Grace Hee, Chair of The Women's Commission,
National Evangelical Christian Fellowship, Malaysia

... beautifully written. I would say it's Papa-written.
I started to read it in McDonald's this morning and couldn't stop. The end of *Eve's Story* is exceptionally powerful;
I began trying not to weep too openly.
Dr Bill Rigden, Founding Asia Director, World Horizons

I love how, while holding to biblical truth,
Joanna reveals fresh insight into how our loving Father relates to his children – especially his daughters
– in our good and our bad moments.
Alison Eckleben, Senior Pastor, Every Nation Church, London

Just read ... in tears ... so awesome. What a Father we have! Can't wait to recommend it to lots of people.
Rebecca Brownridge, Vicar's Wife and Leader, Wales

Wow! I was really impacted by this book. It's not just for women. I think every man serious about his relationship with God should read this, not just to understand the women in his life better, but to have a deeper revelation of God's nature. I'm very very excited to get as many people as possible reading this.
Greg Albrecht, Pastor, Every Nation Church, Slough

It's a great joy to read the result of Joanna's encounter with her heavenly Daddy after receiving Bethel Sozo ministry. In *Forever Loved: Eve's Story,* Joanna retells Eve's life through this new revelation of who Father God is.
Ros Dunlop, Bethel Sozo Team, Bath City Church

… amazing insight into Eve's life. A beautiful story – the language used is incredible. The love of Father, and the delight he has for Eve, even after she sins, is lovely.
Jill Charman, Life Group Leader, Crown Church, London

FOREVER LOVED
EVE'S STORY

A CREATIVE RETELLING

Also by Joanna May Chee

Video Courses

Knowing God: First Steps

Knowing God: Going Deeper

Knowing God: Hear His Voice

Books and Resources

3 Things You Never Knew About Eve:
A Devotional Study

The Cultivate Love Challenge: 50+ Ideas and Resources
to Help Your Family Grow in Love

10 Days | 10 Ways to Meet God in Motherhood

Enjoy 7 Days of Praying for Your Husband

Available at

JoannaMayChee.com

MumsKidsJesus.com

Most are free!

FOREVER LOVED
EVE'S STORY

A CREATIVE RETELLING

Joanna May Chee

Heartfelt
Publications

Forever Loved: Eve's Story
Copyright © 2018 by Joanna May Chee
All rights reserved.

Published by Heartfelt Publications

Design: Joanna May Chee in collaboration with
Rachel Lawston, LawstonDesign.com
Typesetting: Rachel Lawston, LawstonDesign.com

Unless otherwise indicated, all Scripture quotations are taken from the
Holy Bible, New Living Translation, copyright © 1996, 2004, 2007,
2013, 2015 by Tyndale House Foundation. Used by permission of Tyndale
House Publishers, Inc., Carol Stream, Illinois 60188. All rights reserved.

Scripture quotations marked (NIV) are taken from the Holy Bible,
New International Version®, NIV® Copyright © 1973, 1978, 1984, 2011
by Biblica, Inc.® Used by permission. All rights reserved worldwide.

Scripture quotations marked (ESV) are from
The ESV® Bible (The Holy Bible, English Standard Version®),
copyright © 2001 by Crossway, a publishing ministry of
Good News Publishers. Used by permission. All rights reserved.

A CIP catalogue record for this book is available from the British Library.

ISBN 978 1 9998471 0 4 (Paperback)
ISBN 978 1 9998471 1 1 (eBook)

To my wonderful Dad,
Thank you for first showing me the Father love of God.

Contents

Hello!

Thank you for picking up *Forever Loved: Eve's Story*. It's been my dream for years to write a book. I'm thrilled you now hold it in your hands! I pray it blesses you deeply.

I have a gift for you! I'd love to give you my online video course: *Knowing God: Going Deeper*. This 3-day course is for anyone wanting a closer relationship with God, and includes:

- Short videos in which I share my own stories of encountering God (and pray for you to encounter him too).
- Bible studies exploring God's amazing love, his incredible goodness, and hearing God's voice.
- Practical resources to help you meet with God in a fresh way.

Visit
JoannaMayChee.com/deeper
to get the *Knowing God: Going Deeper* course for free.

With love,

Joanna xx

PS. Enjoy the book! I begin by sharing something of my own story, and how this book came to be.

You saw me before I was born.
Every day of my life was recorded in your book.
Every moment was laid out
before a single day had passed.

How precious are your thoughts about me, O God.
They cannot be numbered!

Psalm 139:16-17

Introduction

My Story

'Who wrote this?' my teacher demanded, anger and disbelief filling his voice. My friend looked around, then turned her eyes on me.

'Joanna,' she said.

I was nine years old. I loved school and especially my new teacher, Mr Stanwell. He was the first male teacher I'd ever had, and he was lots of fun. That morning we had free time in class, and I was making a folded paper-thingy – my daughter tells me it's called a chatterbox – you know, the origami-style folded paper with flaps, where you ask someone to choose a colour, then a number, and open and close the flaps accordingly, till you end up with a witty comment like 'You stink!' or 'You love Tommy Biggs!' Lots of amusement for nine-year-old girls! I'd written something in every space but one, and was stuck for another idea.

'What shall I write?' I asked my friends. Lara came up with an idea.

'— —!' she suggested.

I wrote it down. It was a phrase I'd never heard before. I was a good shy Christian girl with no idea it was one of the most offensive things you could ever say to someone.

We had fun playing with my folded chatterbox. A friend asked if she could do it on our teacher. 'Of course!' I replied.

What are the chances?

One-in-eight, actually.

Mr Stanwell chose a colour: open – close – open – close – open – close – open. Mr Stanwell chose a number: open – close – open – close – open. Mr Stanwell chose a flap. My friend opened it up, and read out loud, '— —!'

Mr Stanwell said nothing more about it in class that morning. At lunch time, he called me in from the playground. I remember standing awkwardly with him in the school corridor as he launched into his diatribe: 'I don't care if you use that kind of language at home! I don't care if you use that kind of language on the street! But don't you ever use that kind of language in my classroom! Do you understand?' All I could do was give a small nod as he dismissed me back into the playground.

I didn't tell anyone what had happened.

Over the following months, Mr Stanwell organised lots of fun projects and activities for our class. He appointed students to positions of responsibility – class monitors, library helpers, and playground helpers. I longed to be chosen for something special. My friends were chosen. But Mr Stanwell did not choose me. It hurt.

The years passed. I grew. I forgot. I didn't think about it again.

Thirty years later, I am lying on my bed, eyes closed, thinking about God. In my mind I see the galaxies stretching into the distance. God is out there somewhere, far away in the darkness.

It's not like I don't know God. I do. I've had amazing encounters with him. I've experienced the Holy Spirit working wonders both in me and through me. I know Jesus as my friend.

Now the realisation comes, 'God, I don't know you as Father. You seem so far away.' I pray, 'God, I want to know you as Father. Please show yourself to me.'

Little do I know … this is the beginning.

I had a wonderful relationship with my own father as I was growing up. I remember sitting on his lap, scared because I'd just had my first glimpse of war on the TV. I wondered would my dad have to go away and fight? Arms around me, my dad reassured me that the war was far away. He did not have to go. He would never leave me.

Another time, my 'friends' at school ganged up against me. My dad told me he'd come in and 'sort them out'! My upset faded; my confidence rose. The next day, I boldly told them, 'My dad is coming in to sort you out!' They became my instant friends again!

I remember, as I grew older, sharing deeper things with my dad, enjoying chatting with him about plans and decisions, receiving his counsel and his prayer.

(I still love being with my dad today, chatting and laughing. There's always lots of laughter when my dad's around!)

As the years move on, I wonder, 'Why don't I know God as Father, when I'm so close to my own dad?'

A prayer ministry called Bethel Sozo visits our church.[1] I haven't heard of them before. I'm hungry for more of God. I'm also struggling with deep hurt and disappointment with close relationships gone wrong. I know I need help to forgive and receive God's healing. I sign up for a Sozo prayer session.

I walk into the room, not knowing what to expect. I'm greeted by a lady who introduces herself as Ros. There's a beauty and gentleness about her that reassures me. I sit; Ros gives our time to God, and we begin.

'Close your eyes. I'd like you to imagine yourself in a safe place,' says Ros. 'Where's a safe place for you?'

I see myself sitting beneath a large tree in a meadow. It's beautiful – just me, the tree, flowers, grasses, and a stream. I lean back against the tree, and rest.

'Let's invite God to come,' Ros continues. 'Would you like to invite Father, Son or Holy Spirit to come and be with you?'

'Father God,' I say. I'm so hungry to know him. I want to feel him close. I invite Father God to come and be with me.

'Can you see Father God?' Ros asks. 'Where is he?'

'In the tree, in the branches high above me,' I reply.

Ros leads on, 'Is there anything you want to bring to Father God today?'

I share the disappointment and deep hurt I'm feeling. I share feelings of being misunderstood, unappreciated and labelled. I share my heart to be known for who I really am.

Ros asks me to follow her in prayer, 'Father God, please

show me the first time I felt misunderstood and not known for who I am.'

I repeat the prayer. Immediately I see myself in my classroom all those years ago. I see my friends. I see Mr Stanwell. This memory is so unexpected, so forgotten. I don't know where it comes from. Except I know it comes from God!

I am stunned. God knows. Even when I didn't. I remember more. I see other male authority figures in my life that I've been hurt by. I see a pattern. Always my longing to be known and understood, always my longing for others to take the time to get to know the real me, always my longing to be appreciated and affirmed. I see a pattern. The times I've felt disappointed and let down by male leaders. The times I've hurt so badly when they haven't understood me.

I didn't know. I had no idea. It began with Mr Stanwell. I forgive him now. I release him and the effect he has had on my life. I forgive other male leaders that I've been hurt by.[2]

Ros asks me to give my pain, my hurt to God. I do. She asks me what Father God wants to give me in return. I sit and wait. I hear a word: 'Freedom!'

I hear Father God tell me I'm fun. He wants to climb down the tree and run through the meadow with me. He wants to splash in the stream with me. He wants to get to know me and spend time with me.

Ros leads me on in conversation with my Father. Other words come to me, other pictures. I am not inferior. I am precious. Jesus loves the passion in my heart. He delights in me. I am free. Joy. Excitement. Dancing. I am not afraid of what others think of me.

As the session nears its end, Ros asks me to return to my safe place. I'm sitting again under the tree. Ros asks, 'Where is Father God now?'

I look. He is no longer in the branches of the tree. He is sitting next to me, his arms tight round me. Father God is close, right there, with me.

It takes time to come into the freedom of all God has done in me. The hurt and disappointment try to shoulder their way back in. I learn to keep forgiving, and to keep letting go. I learn to say, 'I have forgiven. Hurt and disappointment, you have no place in me.'

I begin to learn to turn to Father God for love and affirmation, and not to man. It takes time to recognise God's whispered words of love. It takes time to be still and listen out for his voice above all else. It is something I'm still practising, and always will be.

Several months later, I'm lying on a bed again. This time not mine. We're visiting family in Malaysia. Hot, sticky, jet-lagged, I cannot sleep. It's 2 a.m. Words start pouring through my head:

'Hi, I'm your Dad. Wow! You are so beautiful!'
   Arms around me. I look up to see a face swimming with emotion. Eyes, oceans-deep with love for me. A smile, oceans-wide with joy. The voice again, 'You are so beautiful, my precious one. I love you.'

I try to sleep. More words:

'Come away with me. Come away with me, my love.'
   Whispers in my ear. Whispers of love. Whispers of longing.
   Papa takes my hand. We run, we dance, laughing with the joy of our togetherness. Words flow from my Papa's lips,

words of truth, alive, penetrating my deepest being: 'You're so beautiful, precious daughter! I love you! I'm so happy to be with you. Come away with me.'

Finally, at 5 a.m., I admit defeat. I cannot sleep. I get up. I write down all the words that have been flowing through my head. It is the story of Eve. It is the story of a Father's love. It is the story of my Father's love for me.

The next night, the same thing. No sleep. More words. More of the Father's heart for Eve. More of his heart for me. I try to sleep. I cannot. I get up and write it down.

Four nights. More words!

I'm excited. I have a story I did not ask for: Eve's story – one of preciousness and grace. I go back to my Bible. There are things in this story I did not know. There are facets of God's love I could not have imagined. I search my Bible. I ask God. He pours himself out to me.

I write, and gradually, slowly, Eve's story becomes this book.[3]

And so, now, dear friend, as you turn the page and step into Eve's story, I pray you step deep into the Father's love for you. You are his precious daughter.[4] He has loved you from before all time. He whispers to you:

'Come away with me. Come away with me, my love.'

Open up your heart.

As you read, let the Father's words of love to Eve be his words of love to you. Let the Father's heart for Eve be his Father heart for you.

1. Bethel Sozo is a worldwide prayer ministry originating from Bethel Church, Redding, California. 'Sozo' is the Greek word translated 'saved, healed and delivered', and is complete salvation in Jesus. A Sozo session facilitates the individual hearing from Father, Son and Holy Spirit, and receiving inner healing and deliverance. Visit BethelSozo.com or BethelSozo.org.uk for more information.

2. To any male leader reading this: please forgive me for having wrong expectations of you. Forgive me for looking to you for acceptance and affirmation instead of looking to my Father God. I release you to be all God has called you to be. I bless you and love you.

3. This book is an imaginative retelling of Eve's story, based on Genesis 1-5 in the Bible. Eve's story may or may not have happened as I write it. I encourage you to read the Bible account for yourself.

4. I wrote this book as an expression of God's love for women. If you are a male reader, you are just as loved! You are God's precious son. As you continue to read, receive God's love, and substitute male words as necessary.

Eve's Story

1.

I remember the day I was born. No other woman can say that!

Nothingness.

Gradually, a glow, like the first touch of sunrise, then a brightening, a flickering orange behind my eyelids. I open my eyes. Waterfalls of soft light. A voice, as warm and tender as the light on my face, 'Hi, I'm your Dad. Wow! You are so beautiful!'

Arms around me. I look up to see a face swimming with emotion. Eyes, oceans-deep with love for me. A smile, oceans-wide with joy.

The voice again, 'You are so beautiful, my precious one. I love you.'

I describe my birth day with understanding now. At the time, I had no frame of reference to know what I was seeing, or words to describe what I was feeling, though I understood everything my Father said to me. All I knew was that I had not been, and now I was. All I felt was a love so intense it engulfed me.

'My daughter, I love you so much.'

2.

Let me introduce myself a little better. I am Eve, first woman. You and I are related. I am your great – add a few more greats – Grandmother. Maybe one day when we meet, we can sit down together and work out just how many 'greats' there are between us!

You and I are a lot alike, you know. We are sisters too. My Dad is your Dad! If this sounds a little confusing, then I hope things become clearer as I share my story with you.

Let me tell you a little more about my Dad, my Papa. Let me share some more from my birth day:

'Come. Come away with me. Come away with me, my love.'
  Whispers in my ear. Whispers of love. Whispers of longing.
  Papa takes my hand. We run, we dance, laughing with the joy of our togetherness. Words flow from my Papa's lips, words of truth, alive, penetrating my deepest being: 'You're so beautiful, precious daughter! I love you! I'm so happy to be with you. Come away with me.'

  A white dove flies alongside us, riding on my Father's Word, soaring high, diving with delight, finding its place in my heart.

  We come to rest beside still waters. The dove hovers, then settles with us. I enjoy the quiet of the moment, held tight, secure, in my Father's arms.

My Papa, my first love.

'We love because he first loved us.'[1]

1. 1 John 4:19 NIV

3.

'Where's Adam?' you ask. Isn't my story Adam and Eve? Yes, it is. But before that, and even more importantly, my story is one of Father and daughter. It is a story of love, a Father's love so incredible that he created me and desired to be with me. He didn't just make me for Adam you know!

'Come! Come away with me, my love!'

Before anything else, my Dad wanted to love me. He wanted to be with me. He wanted to hold me.

And he was preparing a bride for his son: his son, Adam.

Papa's head turns. I follow his gaze. There in the distance, a figure, bounding over the hillside, coming towards us, seeking us out. My heart leaps. Papa grasps my hand, and, laughing, running, pulls me along towards the stranger.

Joy bubbles up. Love overflows me. I break away from Papa, and call out, words, newly learned, 'Come! Come away with me.'

The white dove soars on my words, high into the clear sky. I call again, louder, 'Come away with me, my love.'

My words and the dove rush together as one, towards the solitary figure.

'The Spirit and the bride say, "Come!"' [1]

1. Revelation 22:17 NIV

4.

Did you ever ask why God didn't just make me at the same time he made Adam? Did you ever wonder why Adam had to search through all the animals looking for a mate, and couldn't find one? Was I just an afterthought?

No! All I knew of in those early days was love and acceptance. I was not an afterthought. As my Father shared his heart with me, I learned of my preciousness. I was a treasure to be sought and found. Adam searched for me excitedly. He longed for me with all his heart. As he named the animals and saw each one with its mate, his desire for me grew and grew. His anticipation of being with me consumed him. He was searching out a bride.

When he found me, I was his greatest treasure.

The lone figure stops, and stares. Delight and wonder fill his face. Then he runs.

'My beloved is mine and I am his.'[1]

1. Song of Songs 2:16 NIV

5.

My wedding was somewhat different from yours, or what you imagine yours will be! I can see your beautiful dress, your amazing flowers. You look stunning. I was stunning too (so Adam told me afterwards). My flowers were exquisite, growing all around me, newly created, aflame with colour and fragrance. My dress? Well, there's the difference. I had no dress! No clothes at all in fact. Adam was dressed likewise. Shocking, I know! My Dad's different like that. He loves freedom. He loves simplicity.

It was a wonderful wedding. Beauty glowed from us!

Papa gave us away to each other. His daughter. His son.

Laughter. Joy. Tears of wonder at this newness of love, discovered today. Papa is with us, smiling, laughing, blessing us:

'Be fruitful and multiply. Fill the earth. Rule and reign. Receive my abundance.' [1]

Our wedding blessing!

And what a blessing: 'Be fruitful and multiply.' You know what that means! There we were, standing beside each other, marvelling at the glory of each other's bodies. What a wedding present! My Dad's something else!

It has always amazed me: our Father having just created us, loving us so much, yet willing to give us away to each other. He didn't cling on to us. He didn't demand we return to him. He let us leave and cleave with each other. He continued to love us just as fiercely as before, but he gave us the choice to return that love.

1. Adapted from Genesis 1:28

6.

Adam and I together, alone, but not alone. The presence of our Father's smile rests on us. A warm breeze gently stirs his words of love in our hearts.

I tremble at my husband's touch. His love, his tenderness, capture me. He has my heart; I give him my all. We delight in each other, revelling in this freedom, this joy, this love so new!

It's fun! I love this husband of mine. We are one.

Lying side by side, hands entwined, we talk, sharing the newness and wonder of our existence.

Sleep comes. We rest in each other's arms, our first wondrous day at an end.

**'Then God looked over all he had made,
and he saw that it was very good!'**[1]

1. Genesis 1:31

7.

And on the seventh day God rested …[1]

What did God do when he rested? Have you ever wondered? Was he so tired from creating that he just went off and slept?

Well, no! My Papa doesn't sleep![2]

So, what did he do? My heart still thrills to remember: he spent the day with us – with me, with Adam.

'Beloved son, precious daughter, come! I want to show you everything I've made for you. Come and see!'

Our Father's voice, excited, calls us to him. Holding hands, Adam and I rise to meet our Papa. Joy rises in my heart. My Papa's smile is infectious. I love being with him. Holding hands with Papa now, we run, we dance, exulting in the glory of new life all around us. Papa shows us wonders beyond description. He shares heart secrets with us. He has waited from before the dawn of eternity for this day, he says. Tears of joy stream down his face as he tells us of our preciousness to him, and his wonder at our now-togetherness.

'Come, come away with me. I have so much to show you, so much to tell you, so much to give you.'

Finally, tumbling together onto the greenest of grass, we catch our breath, and fall in silent awe at our Father's love for us, and the beauty of his creation.

Our first full day: a day of rest with our Father. What a wonderful, amazing thing his rest is!

And this is how it was always meant to be.

---

1. Genesis 2:2
2. Psalm 121:4

8.

Rest. Adam and I were created to enter God's rest.

God could have created us earlier in the week. We could have begun ruling and reigning as our Father created. But no! We were not created to enter his work. We were created to enter his rest. His eternal rest.

Yes, we were called to rule and reign. But this was not work as you know it. It was a joy. It was a privilege. It was a calling that excited us to the depths of our being. The precious creation of our Papa handed over, entrusted, to our care. What an honour! Can you imagine being given the world? It was a gift from our most generous Father. We ruled and reigned, from that place of joyful rest with Papa.

And God? Did he go back to work on day eight? No! His work was done. His desire was to spend the rest of eternity with us, with our children, and with their children. Papa's desire was to share his life, his whole being, his heart … with us … forever.

9.

Let me tell you some more about Eden!

I wish I could share with you in heavenly language. The day will come when you see all and know all. For now, just know that everything I describe is infinitely more beautiful, infinitely more wonderful, and infinitely more incredible than I can ever communicate in human words.

Eden was Beauty. Eden was Life. Beauty and Life pulsated together through every living thing. There was a brilliance, a shine of glory in everything. Trees, plants and flowers radiated colour you have not known: hues of diamond, amethyst, jasper and emerald, to name a few. Every branch, leaf and petal was alive, lifted heavenward, exuding exquisite fragrance, the sweetest of offering. My favourite flower was one of delicate sapphire; small but luxuriant, it grew in its masses by the river side, the translucency of its petals making it almost at one with the shimmering azure of the water. Its scent was a whisper of freshness and goodness.

The hills, the valleys, the rivers, the waterfalls, meticulously crafted, flowed together into a landscape of stunning beauty and delight. Adam and I loved to sit together, soaking in the wonder of our world. Many a time, an animal or two would come and lie beside us, content to be our silent companion, taking pleasure in a back rub or a tummy tickle.

The animals of Eden were wonderful creatures! They were our friends, our playmates, and our help. Can you imagine lying with your head resting in the furry pillow of a lion's mane? Can you imagine playing with elephants in crystal clear water, one elephant squirting you, as another lifts you clear with his trunk? We had such fun! Then there were the small fluffy creatures – the rabbits, the bush babies, the koalas, and suchlike – who loved to snuggle in our laps to be fussed over and petted. There were the monkeys and lemurs that climbed and chattered in the tree tops above us, throwing fruit down to us to feast on. Each animal was special and precious to us, and to our Papa.

And our food – the vegetation and fruit of all that grew around us – it thrilled our every sense. What sights: the iridescent shine of a myriad of brightly coloured fruit, the freshest green of vegetables. What aromas: savoury, sweet, and spice – inviting us to eat. What flavours: each bite, an intricacy, a burst of sensation on our tongues. As we ate, Life spilled through our inmost beings.

Eden was Paradise. A paradise on earth.

10.

Not only did I have a perfect world, I had a perfect husband.

Adam was amazing! We were truly made for each other. Our whole beings complemented and completed each other. Adam romanced and loved me tenderly, and cherished me wholeheartedly. Our marriage was also crazy-fun, joy-filled and full of laughter.

But nothing of the beauty and wonder of Eden, and our love for each other, compared to the beauty and wonder of our Father, and his love.

I began to know Papa not only as Father, but also as Spirit and as Word. His Spirit was ever present, ready to lead and guide, sometimes manifesting as a dove, sometimes as a gentle breeze. Papa's Word was alive, affirming, penetrating my inmost being, bringing truth, and bringing joy.

My Papa was my source, my knowledge, my everything.

In your world, you'd say I had it all. You're right. I did! But, amazingly, my all just kept getting better. Each waking brought new joy and fresh anticipation. Each day brought new intimacies in marriage. Each day I experienced new revelation of my Papa's love for me.

This was Life: Life in all its fullness.

11.

Then.

Death.

12.

'Woman, come.' A voice, strangely sweet yet unfamiliar. I startle awake. 'Come, come with me. I have something to show you.'

I rise, curious, leaving Adam still asleep. The new voice, softly melodious, calls again, 'I have something for you.'

I follow the voice, downwards, through the early morning mist, towards the river. There, by the water's edge, a tree, huge, magnificent, loaded with fruit: the tree of the knowledge of good and evil. It is the one tree I have never eaten from. Papa told us not to. If we eat the fruit, or even touch it, we will die.

I do not know what death is. I know it is something that stirs my Papa's heart in a way nothing else does, in a way I cannot describe or comprehend. But I trust my Papa; I believe his Word and his love for me. I have never touched the fruit, or even looked at it.

Till now.

I look.

There in the branches, a snake, glorious in colour. We have many snakes in Eden; this one outshines them all. I cannot take my eyes off it.

'Woman.' The voice. It is the snake. I stare in wonder. A snake with voice – that is incredible. 'Did God really say you must not eat the fruit from any of the trees in the garden?' [1]

I laugh, 'Of course we may eat fruit from the trees in the garden.' Papa is so good. He has freely given us all things. 'It's only the fruit from this tree in the middle of the garden that we are not allowed to eat. God said, "You must not eat it or even touch it; if you do, you will die."'

'You won't die!' Now it is the snake who laughs.

My heart trembles in a way I have not experienced before. Something in me tells me to look away, but I cannot.

'God knows that your eyes will be opened as soon as you eat it, and you will be like God, knowing both good and evil.'

I love learning from my Papa; I love to be with him. But wouldn't it be amazing to know things for myself. There is so much I do not know. I do not know what death is; I do not know what evil is. I do not understand what stirs my Father's heart when he speaks these words. I want to know. I want to understand.

The fruit looks so good. It is different from any other we have in the garden. I wonder what it tastes like. Surely one bite …

Suddenly – a breeze in my face, gentle at first, then gathering strength – the dove, pure white in the morning light, dips and dives in front of me. I turn to follow its path as it flies over the river and lands in a tree on the other side: the tree of Life. I know this tree well. We eat from it each day. Its fruit is like no other; it is my favourite. Each time I eat of it, Life saturates my very being; passion, joy and freedom overflow me. This fruit makes me alive.

The dove sits there. Beautiful. White. My heart stirs with sudden longing for my Papa, and to eat of Life.

'You will not die!' The snake again. The voice, sweet yet insistent. I turn back. The fruit does look so good. And it offers me knowledge. I can eat from the tree of Life later.

I reach out. I touch the fruit. Nothing happens. I pluck it. I eat.

> **'Today I have given you the choice between life**
> **and death, between blessings and curses ...**
> **Oh, that you would choose life, so that you**
> **and your descendants might live!'**[2]

1. The conversation between the snake and woman is taken from Genesis 3:1-5.

2. Deuteronomy 30:19

13.

The fruit is wonderful. The juice drips down my chin. I must find Adam and give him some. It is delicious. I turn to find him, but he is already there. He has followed me. He has seen all; he has seen me pick and eat. I hold the fruit out to him.

'Try some,' I say. 'It is amazing.' He reaches out and takes it.

At that moment, my stomach twists, and sweet turns to bitter in my mouth. It is the foulest taste, a poison to my heart.

'Adam! No!' I cry.

But it is too late. He has eaten.

Like me, his delight soon turns to pain. He clutches his head and cries out; anguished sobs wrack his body.

What have I done? My mind whirls in confusion and despair.

'Adam!' My distress at seeing my husband, my love, in such torment is greater than the physical pain I feel. Terror seizes me. I rush to Adam's side. How can I help him? What can I do? I reach out to him. But he pushes me away.

Rejection.

Now I know.

I know!

The fruit has brought me knowledge.

I know confusion.

I know fear.

I know rejection.

No one needs to explain these words to me. I know.

'It's all your fault.' The snake is still there, his smile thin and cruel. His words slither round my mind, crushing tighter, tighter. How heavy they feel, but he is right. It is my fault.

Guilt.

Condemnation.

My knowledge increases.

I shiver. I'm cold. This is a new feeling. Then, suddenly, I realise: I am naked. Adam too. I hardly recognise him. The beautiful glow of glory is gone from our bodies.

I try to cover my body with my hands. I feel such shame. The snake leers at me. His gaze molests me. 'How beautiful you are!' he lusts. I know it is not true. I am repulsed by my own body. I am exposed and deeply agitated.

I must get away. I need to hide. I run.

'There is nowhere to run. You belong to me now,' the snake gloats. I hear his voice even as I run. I recognise it now as sickly sweet; it fills me with fear.

14.

Footsteps behind me. Sobbing.

'Wait!'

I turn. Adam runs to join me. I hardly dare to look at him. His nakedness shocks me. His tortured face grieves me. This is not the Adam I know. He stares at me. Embarrassment sweeps over me. What does he think of me now? How unbeautiful I must seem.

Can Adam love me now? How can he? And Papa? I dare not ask it.

Insecurity.

This new feeling takes root deep in my heart, and breaks it into pieces. I can take it no more; I collapse to the ground and weep.

My heart is broken. My world is shattered.

And the sickly whispers continue in my head, 'It's all your fault.'

I know now why Papa warned us not to eat of the tree. But this knowledge comes too late.

15.

'Let's cover ourselves.' Adam speaks, and gestures towards a fig tree growing nearby.

I look up, and notice for the first time how grey it is, how dim. The light of glory has lifted from our world, as well as from our bodies. Colours are dull, and nondescript. Worse than that, leaves and flowers droop earthward, as if in shame. Some lie broken, crushed upon the ground. A new smell rises from the earth to meet me. Decay.

We pick fig leaves and try to stitch them together using reeds and vines. We cover ourselves as best we can. The silence between us is uncomfortable and awkward, just like our new covering.

Finished, we don't know what to do. We sit and wait. For what, we do not know.

16.

In the cool of the evening, we hear footsteps. Gentle. Tentative.

*'Adam, where are you?' The voice of our Father, my Papa.
Joy swells within me at the sound of his voice, but is instantly
crushed by the weight of my guilt. Fear overwhelms me. That
my Papa should see me like this, and know I have done the one
thing he asked me not to.*

*I see the fear rush across Adam's face too. He grabs my hand,
and we run. We hide, in the darkness of the trees.*

'Where are you?'[1] My Father's voice again, calling softly.

*He will find us. There is no point in hiding. Adam takes
a trembling step out from the trees, and replies, 'I heard you
walking in the garden, so I hid. I was afraid because I'm naked.'*

*'Who told you you're naked?' our Father asks. 'Did you eat
the fruit I told you not to?'*

*Adam hesitates, then spews out, 'It was the woman you gave
me who gave me the fruit, and I ate it.'*

*He blames me! Anger rises. Indignation. He saw everything.
He could have stopped me. He could have chosen not to eat.
How dare he blame me? And am I now only the woman that
God gave him, not the one he sought with all his heart? His
words cast blame not only on me, but on our Father.*

*I start forward from the trees, ready to vent my fury on this
man, my once husband.*

Then I see Papa. His eyes, full of tender love, mixed with sorrow, are my undoing. He touches my hair. 'What have you done?' he asks gently. Tears roll down his face.

I can look at him no longer. I fall at his feet. 'The snake deceived me!' I cry out. 'That's why I ate it.'

I too can play the blame game.

---

1. The conversation between God, Adam and the woman is taken from Genesis 3:9-13.

17.

Papa turns to the snake, who has sidled up behind us. 'You are cursed for what you've done! You are cursed more than any animal. You will crawl in the dust as long as you live. There will be hatred between you and the woman, and your child and hers. He will crush your head, and you will strike his heel.' [1]

I look up. Papa speaks with such power and authority. And in his voice, there is a ring of promise and of triumph that I do not understand.

Papa speaks again, this time to me. His words are softer, filled with sadness. 'Your pregnancy will be difficult, and birth a terrible struggle. You will want to control your husband, but he will rule over you.'

Then to Adam, he continues, 'You listened to your wife, not me. You ate the fruit I told you not to. Now the ground is cursed because of you. All your life, you'll struggle to work the land. It will produce thistles and thorns. It's only by hard sweat you'll get enough grain to eat. You'll labour in dust until you return to it.'

And so, our wedding blessing turned to cursing. The tragedy was not ours alone, as well you know. The tragedy was all mankind's. It is too little too late to say these words, but I am sorry, so very sorry.

1. God's words to the snake, Adam and the woman are adapted from Genesis 3:14-19.

18.

And yet, that's not the end. My Papa had a plan!

In the midst of death, darkness and despair, God spoke victory. In the midst of cursing, he spoke hope … through me!

I did not fully grasp it at the time – I was overwhelmed with shame and guilt; even in the years to come, the full mystery was hidden from my sight. But Papa promised hope: a saviour was to come; he would crush the serpent's head, and bring forth Life.

It still amazes me. I weep at Papa's love.

I fell; he sought me out.

I fell; he loved me.

I fell; he chose me. He chose my future child, to bring his victory.

That's my Papa for you. His grace is outrageous. He's one cool and loving Dad!

19.

Adam takes my hand, and pulls me up. Still naked, but for the fig leaves, we stand before our Father, our sin exposed, our future laid before us bleak and heavy.

Adam turns to me to speak. More accusation? I expect it, and deserve it. But no! In his voice, I hear an echo of my Father's triumph: 'Your name shall now be Eve.' [1]

I did not expect that. Adam changed my name. He called me Eve! Do you know what that spoke to me, right there, in my darkest moment, when I expected words of blame and hate?

Eve means Life, source of Life, and mother of many. Like my Papa, Adam spoke of Life to come, and he spoke it over me.

Eve: that name is precious to me. It holds the love of my husband; he chose me as the mother of his children, and renamed me. It holds the love of my Father, a new start, and the promise of a saviour.

1. Genesis 3:20

20.

Blazing light!

In our Father's hand, a sword shines bright. I am swallowed by new fear. Is this the end then; is this now death? It is all that I deserve.

Suddenly, into the clearing, there comes a lamb, pure spotless white. Papa steps towards the lamb and gently takes its head. The sword glides down, across its neck.

'No!' I scream. Face in hands, I sob. 'Why?' I cry out. 'Why?'

This lamb, so precious to our Papa – his new creation – lies before us, dead.

**' "Behold, the Lamb of God, who takes
away the sin of the world!" '**[1]

---

1. John 1:29 ESV

21.

First woman. First to sin. First to experience God's mercy and his grace.

Papa took that lamb and made clothes for us from its wool and skin.

I shiver. What is Papa doing? There is blood everywhere. I have backed up into the undergrowth, half-hidden, not wanting to watch, but curiosity getting the better of me. I still cannot believe the lamb is dead.

'Come, Eve,' Papa calls to me.

My new name; it sounds warm on his voice, and stirs longing in my heart. For a moment I forget the terror of the day, and just want to run into my Papa's arms. Then remembrance comes, and I shrink back.

Papa holds out the fleecy lamb skin, white, and somehow clean of blood. 'Come, Eve,' Papa whispers softly.

I know he wants to clothe me. I know he still cares for me. But I cannot move. It's safe here. It's dark. I'm hidden. If I move, he'll see my nakedness, my shame. The fig leaves do not cover much. I know I am no longer beautiful.

It is my choice, I know. Longing: I want to run to him. Fear: I dare not.

A movement. I glance up. Papa is walking towards me. He smiles and holds the lamb skin out to me again. He is offering me a gift. And, somehow, I know that it is more than clothes. Papa's love overwhelms me. I run out, crying, longing, into his arms.

The lamb skin, warm around me, I look up into the eyes of my Dad, my Papa, my first love. They are full of joy, and of delight. He holds me to him. 'You are so beautiful, my precious one. I love you,' he says.

Forgiven. Accepted. Beautiful.

The fig leaves lie at my feet, forgotten. A soft breeze blows in my face: the dove. I haven't seen him since I ate.

'But God demonstrates his own love for us in this: While we were still sinners, Christ died for us.'[1]

1. Romans 5:8 NIV

22.

Adam, too, chose to step out of darkness, and let Papa clothe him.

Do you know what a moment in history that was? Adam and I standing there clothed in white, held in the embrace of our loving Father.

I think, over the ages, the sin has become greater than the redemption. Adam and I are remembered for the wrong we did, not for the saving love of our amazing Father. Papa told me later that the heavens, and all heavens' angels, danced in joy that moment – the moment that we let our Father clothe us.

Salvation's plan was put in place.

23.

I was nervously shy of Adam in his new clothing when I first dared look at him, though relieved I could do so without embarrassment. I was uncertain of his feelings for me, not sure of where I stood, glad of Papa's hand in mine.

The future too was unclear. It was a new beginning, one filled with apprehension and uncertainty.

'Adam, Eve, come, you have to leave.'

Papa tells us we can no longer eat from the tree of Life. He doesn't want us to live forever in this fallen world. He has a greater plan than that.

Hand in hand, Papa in the middle, we walk to the edge of Eden. From the faded beauty of our garden, we stare out onto a land desolate and bare. From dust we came. To dust we now return.

Papa walks with us out into the desert land. I find comfort in his presence.

'For I am convinced that neither death nor life, neither angels nor demons, neither the present nor the future, nor any powers, neither height nor depth, nor anything else in all creation, will be able to separate us from the love of God that is in Christ Jesus our Lord.'[1]

1. Romans 8:38-39 NIV

24.

Our new life began. It was strange and difficult, foreign to all we were used to.

The ground was barren, hard and dry, conquered only by our sweat and tears. Our marriage too was an arid land, equally difficult to tend, the luscious blooms of love and tenderness that once flourished, now lay bruised and crushed, crowded by weeds of uncertainty and fear.

It took time. Much time.

Surely, slowly, the land yielded to our care, each handful of produce a hard-earned blessing. Surely, slowly, we learned new love for each other. It was a love easily torn down by words of anger, frustration and of pain. But it was a love birthed in Eden, too precious to let go of.

We did not see the serpent again, but his whispers lived on in the hardness of the soil and the darkness of the night.

Fear. Guilt. Anger. Shame.

At times these overwhelmed me. Other times, it was with anguish that I thought on all we'd lost.

Only years later did I see the full effect of our first sin, not just our loss, but the pain of all mankind: jealousy, hatred, murder, strife and war. A heavy burden to bear responsibility for, and one that would have been too much to bear. I couldn't have, and nor could Adam.

So, again, I tell you of my Papa ...

25.

He was there. He never left us.

Yes, it was different now. We did not always see him so clearly, or hear him so certainly. It was a choice to hear his words of love and acceptance, of forgiveness and hope, to believe his truth over the whispered lies of the evil one. It was a choice to remember the sacrifice he made for us, and not the sin.

There were days and seasons I did not hear him, or choose to look for him, so caught up as I was in my own sorrows. But, gently, lovingly, he drew me to himself, again and again, and as time went on I learned to live in his presence, day by day.

I still failed. I still sometimes listened to the lies. But Papa's love was unchanging, his acceptance complete. I could run, at any time, into my Daddy's arms.

As Adam and I grew in our healing and wholeness, we determined to keep alive the memory of Eden, and the garden now sealed from us by mighty angels and a flaming sword. We determined to keep alive the memory of what Papa did for us when he clothed us and forgave us.

We determined to tell the generations to come of the amazing goodness of our Father, beginning with our sons.

26.

Our first was Cain, born into our early days of challenge in our new and barren land. He was precious to me, my first born.

In the days leading up to his birth my curiosity overwhelmed me. What would a miniature Adam and Eve look like? I had seen baby animals before but never a baby of our kind. Thankfully, I had seen animals give birth and suckle their young, otherwise I would not even know how this baby of mine was going to come into the world, or survive.

The birth of Cain was filled with uncertainty and travail. I did not know what was happening or how long it would go on for. Adam was a lone and first-time midwife, ill-prepared to help in any way. In my desperate moments, I cried out to my Papa, and felt him come with comfort and with peace.

It was with Papa's help that this little babe came into our bare bleak world. He was beautiful: first baby, first child, first man born of flesh and not of dust. I loved him tenderly. Secretly, I wondered, 'Is he the one who will one day crush the serpent's head?'

Cain grew, knowing our deep loss, seeing our struggles, helping us to tame the wild land. It saddened me greatly to see the stoop of his shoulders as he worked the hot dry land. Adam's curse was now his curse, without him ever having known the blessing.

27.

Our second son was Abel. He was a joy and my delight, my second tiny human blessing.

As our boys grew, and as Adam and I grew in certainty of our Father's forgiveness and acceptance, we told them of Eden and our beginnings, the joy, the wonder, then our sin and our remorse. We shared with them the love of Papa, and rejoiced as they too gradually came to know him.

Each season, we brought choice lambs, the best we had, and sacrificed them in remembrance of Life given for us, the Life that clothed us, covering our nakedness and shame. We came in thankfulness of heart, and taught our boys to do the same.

Cain and Abel grew in statue and in strength. Abel's love of animals led him to care for the flocks and herds we gradually accrued, while Cain continued to work the rocky ground.

My boys, I loved them both so very much. They were my world, my help, my blessing.

28.

I did not know, or else I may have seen it coming.

I did not know there could be such a jealousy. I did not know that bitterness could take such root.

I did not know one man could kill another.

I did not know my son could kill his brother.

29.

'Boys, come. Are you ready? Let's go.'

Joy fills my heart. It's a day of sacrifice. A day of thankfulness to Papa. I love these days. God's Spirit falls as we lift our thanks and praise to him. His love engulfs me, and I am swept back into the garden of his presence. It's a wondrous time, the closest I ever get to being back in the garden with my Daddy.

'Boys, come. Your father's waiting.'

'I'm not coming.'

Shocked, I turn.

Cain. Silent and defiant.

'Why?'

No answer.

'Come on Cain. Let's go.'

'I told you. I'm not coming.'

'Cain!'

'Why should I?' he explodes, his voice filled with a sardonic hardness I have not heard before. 'I don't want to give thanks to your God. He's done nothing for me!'

'Cain …'

'No! I work this ground so hard. Every single day. I'm sick of it. I'm tired of it all. I hate hearing of your life before. I never knew Eden and I never will, so don't go on about it. Life's hard enough, without knowing just how good it was for you. And

Abel, he doesn't do a thing to help. He has it easy, doesn't he? Tending those precious sheep of his. I wish I had it so easy. But no, there's just too much hard ground out there, isn't there? If this is life, I hate it. I wish I'd never been born.'

'Cain ...' I reach out.

'No, don't touch me!'

And with a crushing, 'And you know what? If you had just listened to your precious Papa in the first place ...' he storms away.

30.

'Come on. What's keeping you?' Adam comes looking for us. 'Where's Cain?'

'Adam ...' I begin. I cannot finish. My throat constricts; my words choke me.

'Cain doesn't want to come.' Abel speaks for me.

'I'll go get him,' Adam says. 'We sacrifice together, as a family.'

It's with heavy heart I give this sacrifice.

Abel brings two lambs, beautiful and white, and bows in worship and surrender, his heart burdened for his brother, but his face lifted to his Father. Cain brings a sheath of grasses, torn hastily, from the looks of them, from the field-side. He neither bows, nor lifts his hands in worship. He leaves as quickly as he can.

I kneel before my Papa. I feel his soft touch upon my head. I weep quietly, but my heart cries out in pain.

31.

'Where's Abel? Where's Cain?' I have seen neither of them since the sacrifice.

'I don't know,' says Adam. 'I'll go and look for them.'

Fear.

I'm not sure why. Another emotion added to my day.

Rejection: my son hates me, my love for Papa, and all that I have taught him.

Accusation: my son blames me for the hardness of his life.

Guilt: he's right; it is my fault.

It cuts deep.

Oh, Papa, why? What could I have done differently? How could I have loved him more? How can he turn from you? You're so good.

And then I remember. It's what I did, and Adam too. The pattern has been set in place.

32.

Footsteps. Heavy. Slow.

It's Adam. Alone.

And then I know.

Gone. Both of them.

One dead.

The other missing.

33.

'Eve, come. Come away with me.'
Whispers of love. Whispers of joy.
'Eve, come.'
I wake. It's been so long. Papa's voice pulls on my heart.
'I love you, my beautiful one.'
I weep. Helpless. Hopeless.

And so, my Papa loved me. He came in my grief. He wiped my tears and held me.

34.

We searched for Cain, and heard word of him far east of Eden, in the Land of Wandering.

I longed to see him again as my son.

'Cain, why? You know we loved you. You know we cared. I'm sorry life was what it was for you. I didn't know how you felt. I didn't know how much you hurt. Oh, Cain … come back to us.'

I dreaded to meet him as the murderer of Abel.

'Abel, my precious son. I miss you so much. Abel, I wish I could hold you and tell you how much I love you …'

My emotional dilemma was given answer: Cain did not want to see us.

Over the years, the fame of Cain and his family spread.[1] My heart stored each piece of news, and took silent pride in all my son's achievements. Cain founded a great city. His descendants made wonderful discoveries. My heart gave grateful thanks for God's protection and favour on Cain's life.

But other news distressed me deeply. Cain's descendants took wives just as they pleased. They grew in arrogance and pride. Murder was something they boasted of. The name of God did not exist.

It broke my heart. And it broke Papa's.

1. Genesis 4:17-24

35.

Seth. God gave me another son, one born from broken hearts made one again. He was my joy, my consolation, my little Adam.

Seth's likeness to Adam really was incredible. I wish you could have seen them together, baby and father, both stirring new love and hope in me: a new beginning, a second chance at doing right.

Other children, sons and daughters, followed. We shared the work between us, making sure no one was overburdened, gladly helping each other, sharing the love of Papa as we did so.

Our tribe grew.

It may seem strange to you today, but our children married each other. Our blood was pure, and God's blessing was on our children's marriages. All changed in later years as man walked further from God's ways of love, and human blood became increasingly defiled.

Can you imagine our great joy, watching our children getting married, not to strangers but to ones so dear? Soon, there was a multitude of grandchildren, nephews, nieces, cousins, then great-grandchildren, grand-nieces, -nephews, -cousins. Many of our great-great-grandchildren were older than our own children, we lived so long! It was a wonderful mix of generations and of joy.

We spread. We grew. We began to fulfil God's original blessing to multiply and fill the earth. It delighted us. It delighted Papa.

Seth married one of our beautiful daughters, and bore a son, Enosh, the first grandchild to live near us. How precious to see my grandson grow, the first child to know the blessing of uncles, aunts, and grandparents.

What thrilled my heart more than anything was to see my children and my grandchildren drawing close to Papa. His presence covered our family. Life, once more, was filled with laughter. We acknowledged God, and his provision was abundant. It was incredible to come together as family in worship and thanksgiving, and feel the smile of Papa rest upon us, to hear his voice, not just to me:

'Come. Come away with me.'

The generations truly began to know and worship Papa.[1]

1. Genesis 4:26

36.

The years passed. Hundreds of them. The generations spread far and wide. I mourned the news of peoples lost in great debauchery. I rejoiced at news of peoples who clung to Papa, and revered his name. Among them was one very special little boy: Enoch.

'Nana, tell me again. Tell me about Eden.'

'Well, my precious one. It was amazing. I walked with Papa every day. I knew him like a real person. We used to play with the animals together. They weren't frightened of us, you know.'

'Can I see God like you used to see him, Nana? I want to see Papa God. I want him to show me the animals and the birds and everything he made.'

'Well, my sweetie. God is with us, every day. I don't see him quite as I used to, but I feel him. I know his love. I talk with him each day.'

'I want to see Papa like you did, Nana. I want to walk with him, like you did, in real life.'

'Oh, Enoch, ask him! Ask him to come and be with you. Ask him to come and talk with you. Ask him to walk with you. He loves you so much.'

And so, he did.[1]

1. Genesis 5:21-24

37.

Enoch. Precious child. His hunger challenged me. I wanted more of Papa too.

I began to seek Papa afresh, asking him to come to me as he had done in the garden. I lay quietly awake at night, searching for his face, then seeing it, tender, his eyes full of love for me, his smile full of infectious joy.

Papa drew closer. I drew closer too. Then, one morning, I did not open my eyes to the fresh dawn of day.

Dazzling light.

A voice full of thunder.

'O death, where is your victory? O death, where is your sting?' [1]

The voice again, this time gentle, warm, 'Eve …'

My heart thrills. Papa!

Hands held out to me. Nail pierced. Word become flesh.

A breeze caresses my hair and lifts my heart. His Spirit, a dove.

A face full of tender emotion. My Father, my Papa. Tears of love spilling down his cheeks.

'Come, Eve, my beautiful one. Come and be with me. Forever.'

1. 1 Corinthians 15:55

In Closing

Your Story

There is a word used often in the Psalms: Selah. Its true meaning is uncertain. It seems to indicate a pause to stop and consider what's just been read (or in the case of the Psalms, sung). I like this transliteration of the word:

Selah: pause to carefully weigh the meaning of what we have just read, lifting up our hearts in praise to God for His great truths.[1]

If you haven't already, take a moment now to pause and reflect on *Eve's Story*. Let Father God call you to him. Let him wrap his arms around you. You are his cherished daughter. He's been thinking precious thoughts about you from before all time.

Selah.

I don't know what your story is, but God does, and he cares. His heart has always been to know you, and be with you. Life may have told you otherwise. Earthly relationships may have coloured your view of God, as they did mine. But he comes now gently to hold you close and whisper, 'My beautiful one. The one I cannot do without. I love you. You are mine.'

There is no failure, there is no sin, there is no mess too great for God to step in. Nothing you have done, nothing that has happened to you, disqualifies you from his love. He just can't help himself. He's in love with you. Passionately. Head-over-heels. Crazy-in-love.

He delights to be with you!

He loves to run through the meadows with you. He loves to dance with you. It thrills his heart to see your smile, and hear your voice.

He loves to come, even in your darkest moments, as he did to Eve, never condemning, always loving. He calls you from your hiding place and covers your shame with grace and mercy. He gently touches your hair, and whispers hope and life to you. He holds your hand as you walk through desert places.

He is faithful God. He is unchanging Father. Your circumstances, or how you feel, do not determine his actions, his thoughts toward you, or his love.

He longs to take you deeper. There is so much more of him.

He will never leave you nor forsake you.[2]

You are forever loved.

1. GotQuestions.org/selah.html

2. Deuteronomy 31:8

A Prayer to Receive God as Father

If you'd like to ask God to be a part of your life, or you want to rededicate your life to him, then I invite you to pray the following prayer:

Father God,

I want to know you. I want to know you as Eve did. Thank you for seeking me out, tenderly, lovingly. Thank you for coming to me in my guilt and shame. I'm sorry for hiding from you. Forgive me. Thank you for shedding blood for me. Thank you for sending Jesus to die for me that I might live. I receive you now. Clothe me in white. Speak a new name over me, a new future, a new hope. Thank you I'm forgiven. Thank you I'm accepted. Thank you I am loved. I choose to walk with you, hand-in-hand, wherever that may take me. Thank you for being with me.

Amen.

If you have prayed this prayer, then know that God now lives with you, and in you. His arms are forever around you. He will never let you go. Just as Eve was born into God's love, you have been 'born again' into God's love. Heaven rejoices over you. The angels are celebrating! Your Father, your Papa, smiles on you!

To help you on your journey with God, I'd love to give you my free online resource *Knowing God: First Steps*. This resource includes a short video and information explaining more of the decision you've made to know God, what to do next, and practical ways to get to know him.

Visit

JoannaMayChee.com/first-steps
to get the *Knowing God: First Steps* course for free.

A Prayer for More of God

If you long for more of God, or want to know him closer, then I invite you to pray the following prayer:

Dear God,

I'm hungry for more of you. I long to know you as Eve did, to hear your whispers of love, to feel your arms round me. I want to know you as Father. Come and fill me anew. Overflow me. I want to walk with you, run with you, dance with you! Take me deeper. I'm sorry for the times I drift away, when I let whispered lies replace your truth. Light a fire in me again. Papa, Jesus, Holy Spirit, stir a passion in my heart for you. Come today. I want to meet you.

Amen

If this is your prayer, then know that God hears, and responds. Take a few moments to rest in him and receive all he wants to pour into you and over you. Expect more of him in the days ahead. Keep asking. Keep coming. Keep receiving.

To help you go deeper in your relationship with God, I'd love to give you my free online course: *Knowing God: Going Deeper*. This 3-day course includes:

- Short videos in which I share my own stories of encountering God (and pray for you to encounter him too).

- Bible studies exploring God's amazing love, his incredible goodness, and hearing God's voice.
- Practical resources to help you meet with God in a fresh way.

I had a lot of fun creating this course. God touched me with laughter and tears! I pray he touches you too!

Visit

JoannaMayChee.com/deeper
to get the *Knowing God: Going Deeper* course for free.

Thank You!

Dear Reader,

Thank you for reading *Forever Loved: Eve's Story*.

My heart's desire is for the message of this book to reach women around the world, women who are hurting, women who have never heard God loves them, women who just simply want to know God more.

Can you do two things for me to help this book reach others?
- Leave a short review on Amazon or Goodreads. (Visit JoannaMayChee.com/review for details of how and where to leave reviews.)
- Share this book with your friends. (Use one of the social sharing buttons at JoannaMayChee.com/eve to share via Facebook, Twitter, Pinterest or email.)

Thank you so much! I pray God uses this book to speak his love to many, and continues to reveal himself to you.

Joanna xx

PS. You'll find sample chapters of *Forever Loved: Eve's Story: The Devotional Bible Study* (the companion guide to *Forever Loved: Eve's Story*) at the end of this book.

About the Author
Joanna May Chee

Photo Credit: David Chee

I'm married to an amazing man, and have four incredible kids! We've lived (and had many adventures) in Malaysia, Bosnia and Turkey, and are now settled in Slough, just outside of London.

I get excited about God. I love to write. I'm often awake in the night with a million ideas for my next book or course. It's my heart to encourage and equip women to love their families and meet with God. There's so much more of him!

Visit my websites to find out more; and subscribe to receive blog posts, free resources, and news of future books:

JoannaMayChee.com • MumsKidsJesus.com

I also hang out (or try to) on:

Facebook.com/JoannaMayChee
Facebook.com/MumsKidsJesus
Pinterest.com/MumsKidsJesus

See you soon!

The Knowing God Video Series

by Joanna May Chee

Available online at
JoannaMayChee.com/courses

Some courses are free!

Check out the companion guide to
Forever Loved: Eve's Story

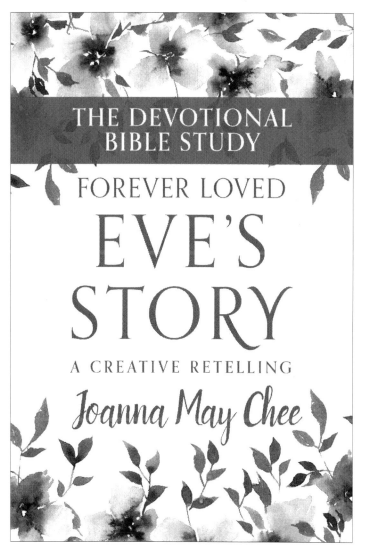

JoannaMayChee.com/eve-devo

Carry on reading for the first three chapters …

Forever Loved: Eve's Story
The Devotional Bible Study

How to use this devotional study:

- Before each study, pray and ask God to speak to you.
- Work through each section – Think About – Discover – Apply – Pray.
- Use a Bible, where needed, to answer the questions. If you don't have access to a Bible, you can use an online version such as BibleGateway.com
- Write down your answers to each question. If you don't want to write in this book, use a notebook, or download a free printable version of the sample chapters here: JoannaMayChee.com/devo-sample

Note: The optional Extra Book Study at the end of each day, includes analysis of the relevant chapter in *Eve's Story*, and extra questions for thought.

Enjoy!

Day 1: Born into Love

Think About

How do you think Eve spent her first moments of life?

Who did Eve first see when she was created?

Discover

Read Genesis 2:18-22. What clues do these verses give to the questions above?

God **brought** Eve to Adam! This must mean that Eve was with God first. Imagine, Eve waking to new life, waking to the presence of God, waking to see the face of her Father smiling upon her!

Of course, we don't know how long God spent with Eve before bringing her to Adam. I like to think he spent at least a little time delighting in her, loving her, thrilling at his beautiful creation. Imagine how amazing it must have been for God to hold his first daughter in his arms!

The following verses reveal God's love for his children throughout history. With reference to these verses, how do you think God **feels** about Eve at her creation?

Zephaniah 3:17

Jeremiah 31:3

Psalm 139:13-18

Song of Songs 1:15

Romans 5:5b

Ephesians 1:3-6

Ephesians 3:17b-19

1 John 3:1

With reference to the previous verses, what do you think
God might **say** to Eve in her first few moments of life?

Apply

Look again at what you've written in the *Discover* section. This is not just what God may have felt about Eve. This is not just what God may have said to Eve.

This is what God **feels** about you! This is what God **says** to you!

This is God's truth about you!

Maybe you knew love at birth. Maybe you didn't. Maybe you knew love growing up. Maybe you didn't. Maybe you know love now. Maybe you don't.

The wonderful thing is, whatever your life's circumstances, there is a second chance at birth. There is a second chance at love. Yes! You can be born again … into a love like no other, not in the natural sense of course, but in a spiritual sense. You can start your life afresh with God. Ask him to come and give you a new start. Give him your life. Be born again into his love. Know him holding you. Hear him say, 'You are so beautiful my precious one. I love you.'

If you'd like to ask God to be a part of your life, and be born into his love, you can use the prayer on page 103 of this book.

Maybe you have already been born again into God's love. That's wonderful! You too can experience God's love anew today. He has so much more for you!

Read *Forever Loved: Eve's Story*, **Chapter 1**. As you do, imagine waking afresh to the love of Father God today. Rest in his arms. Hear him whisper his love to you.

He delights in being with you, his precious daughter.

Pray

Dear Father,

Thank you for loving me so much. It's amazing how you pour your love out on me, how you smile on me, how you delight in me. I long for more of you. Help me know you as Eve did. I want to wake to your presence anew today.

Amen.

Listen to my message *Eve: Loved and Accepted* for more revelation of God's love for Eve, and God's love for you:

JoannaMayChee.com/speaking

Extra Book Study

1. Note down the phrases and imagery used to describe Father God in *Forever Loved: Eve's Story*, **Chapter 1**:

His presence:

His voice:

His words:

His arms:

His face:

His eyes:

His smile:

His love:

2. Does this match the God you know?

3. What is your response to him?

Day 2: No Other Voices

Think About

What is more true: what God thinks about you, or what you think about yourself?

Discover

Look again at what you wrote for the verses listed in the *Discover* section of Day 1. These words are from the Bible. They are truth. God's truth! About you.

What do the following verses tell us about God's word?

Psalm 12:6

Psalm 33:4

Isaiah 40:8

John 1:1-4

Ephesians 6:17

Hebrews 4:12

1 Peter 1:23-25

Apply

Before the Fall, Eve lived in total truth. No lies. No doubt. No insecurity. She lived totally in who God said she was. There was nothing else to believe. There were no other voices!

Write some 'I am' truths about yourself using the following Bible verses from Day 1. (You may be able to write more than one thing for each verse.)

Jeremiah 31:3 I am ...

Psalm 139:13-18 I am ...

Song of Songs 1:15 I am ...

Ephesians 1:3-6 I am ...

Imagine this to be total truth. Imagine this to be the **only** truth about you. No lies. No doubt. No other voices.

The amazing reality is: this is **the truth**, the only truth about you. You don't just have to imagine it!

Speak these 'I am' truths out loud. Let God's truth sink into your heart and transform your mind.

Read *Forever Loved: Eve's Story*, **Chapter 2**. As you do, let Father God call you to him. Let his words of truth find their place in your heart. God longs to be with you.

Enjoy his presence. Rest secure in him.

Pray

Father,

Thank you that you are **truth***. I choose to live in your truth, and what you say about me. Help me to recognise other voices and speak your truth over them. I want to live in your presence as Eve did.*

Amen.

Extra Book Study

1 John 4:19 is quoted at the end of *Forever Loved: Eve's Story*, **Chapter 2**: 'We love because he first loved us.'

1. How does this verse apply to Eve's story so far? (Remember, Eve hasn't met Adam yet.)

2. How does this verse apply to your life?

Eve lived in the presence of Father, Son and Holy Spirit.

3. How are Father, Son and Holy Spirit present in *Forever Loved: Eve's Story*, **Chapter 2**?

4. Read the following verses to see how this ties in with scripture:

Genesis 1:1-3

John 1:1-5

John 1:14

Luke 3:21-22

5. How are Father, Son and Holy Spirit present in your life?

Day 3: Created to Be

Think About

Why did God create Eve?

Discover

Read the following verses. What clues do they provide to the question above?

Genesis 2:18-25

Genesis 1:26-28

Can you think of any other reasons why God created Eve?

Why do you think God created you?

What did God create you for, according to the following verses?

Ephesians 2:10

Jeremiah 29:11

Matthew 28:18-20

These verses are primarily what God created us **to do**. They are wonderful verses. We are created with purpose, wonderful purpose. God has a destiny for us, and it is a good one.

And, yet, there's more! God didn't just create us **to do**; he created us **to be**.

Read the following verses, and note down what we are created **to be**:

1 John 3:1

Ephesians 1:3-14

Romans 8:14-17

Isaiah 54:5

Revelation 19:7-9

Wow! What an amazing list. We're chosen and adopted to be God's children. We're heirs of God, and co-heirs with Christ. We are the bride of Christ. Ultimately, we are created to have the most intimate relationship possible. With God! We are part of his family, and he can't get enough of us!

Apply

God loves a good love story! He created us to be romanced; he created us to belong. He sent Jesus to woo our hearts. He wants us to fall desperately in love with him.

Read *Forever Loved: Eve's Story*, **Chapter 3**. As you do, let the Holy Spirit kindle a fresh longing in your heart for Father and Son. Let your heart response be, 'Amen. Come Lord Jesus.' Revelation 22:20 NIV.

Yearn for him. Hunger for him. He will come.

If you feel weary, or have lost your desire for God, come to him in honesty. Tell him how you feel. Ask his help. Let him spark fresh desire in your life.

Remember: 'We love because he first loved us.' 1 John 4:19 NIV.

Let him love you.

Pray

Thank you, Father, for choosing me to be a part of your amazing family. Thank you for wanting me. Thank you for knowing me. I want to be a part of your love story. I long to be romanced. I want to fall in love with your son, Jesus. Take me deeper into you.

Amen.

Extra Book Study

1. In *Forever Loved: Eve's Story*, **Chapter 3** what role does the Father play in preparing Eve for Adam?

2. What does Adam do?

3. How does the Spirit help bring Adam and Eve together?

Note: Forever Loved: Eve's Story *is an imaginative retelling of the Bible account. It may not have happened like this. But it's a lovely picture of how Father, Son and Spirit work together to woo and love us.*

Adam and Eve are representative of Christ and his bride (us).

4. How do you think Father, Son and Holy Spirit work together in wooing and loving you?

5. Do you have a part to play?

6. What are the roles of Father, Son and Holy Spirit in the following verses? And your role?

John 3:16

1 John 3:1a

1 John 4:19

Luke 19:10

Song of Songs 2:8-14

Romans 8:15-16

Revelation 22:17, 20

Isn't it amazing how Father, Son and Spirit work together, and on each other's behalf?

7. What is your response?

Did you enjoy this devotional sample?

Visit

JoannaMayChee.com/eve-devo
to be notified of the publication of
Forever Loved: Eve's Story: The Devotional Bible Study

Order discounted bulk copies
Forever Loved: Eve's Story for your
church, group or event.

Visit
JoannaMayChee.com/bulk-orders

Acknowledgements

Many thanks to…

Esther Waldrop: for being the first person to read *Eve's Story*. You encouraged me so much, and helped me believe this book could really happen! Thank you too for your invaluable editing advice.

Ros Dunlop: for sozo-ing me (twice), and for your gentle, loving ministry. This book comes largely from what God did in me through you.

Bill and Sarah Rigden, Greg and Suzanne Albrecht, and Maggie Avery: for reading the draft copy of this book, and giving invaluable feedback. Your friendship and support are precious to me.

Anna San Jose: for stepping in last minute when I needed an editor, proofreader and friend. You did an amazing job, made some great suggestions, and encouraged me immensely!

My mum, Caroline Quinton: for working through the sample devotional chapters, checking every Bible reference, and making sure it all made sense. You did a brilliant job!

Rachel of LawstonDesign.com: for taking my design and creating an amazing cover, and for making the inside of this book so beautiful. I'm glad I found you!

My reviewers: for taking the time to read *Forever Loved: Eve's Story*, and write such nice things! I appreciate you very much.

My launch team: for believing in me, and your amazing support and willingness to share this book with the world.

Annakarin Steen, Teri Pithey, Negar Eghtessadi-Reed, and Megs Crummack: for being special friends. You were with me, and alongside me, in the difficult days when this book was birthed. I am forever grateful for your friendship. I miss you.

My wonderful family at Every Nation Church, Slough: for your enthusiastic support and affirmation. I love your passion for Jesus, and I'm excited to 'keep going' with you!

Pa and Aunty Teresa: for being lovely parents-in-law, and for the gentle presence of God in your lives and in your home. My jet-lagged nights in your house is where this story began!

My amazing husband, Lawrence: for never doubting (even when it took so long)! You have been incredible, always supporting, always encouraging, always providing what I needed to make this book happen. You mean so much to me.

My fantastic kids – Josh, Dave, Sam and Miriam: for getting excited with me about this book, and asking the important questions like how much longer till it's published, and how much money it's going to make! Special thanks, too, Dave for your great photography!

Printed in Great Britain
by Amazon